YEARS

A 10 STEP GUIDED JOURNAL TO HELP YOU BREAK FREE FROM FEELING STUCK FOR YEARS!

LATOSHA NICOLE

To:_____

From_____

Date:_____

Hey Boo!

As I share my experiences and you work through this journal, I want you to know I've prayed for your faith to be strengthened, your purpose to be revealed and that God moves suddenly in your life. Journaling is a way that you RELEASE emotions, ease stress and will allow you to connect with God and YOURSELF on a whole different level! So, this 10 step Journal is a start to guide you through any uncertain days, to encourage, inspire, uplift and share what allowed and is still allowing me to be a bolder version of myself. Be prepared to be different. Chilllleeee let's not waste another YEAR feeling stuck, let's put in the action and expect more! Your breakthrough is coming, grab a pen and let the journaling begin.

Your New Friend Nikki

To My future grandkids

Proverbs 13:22 says "a good man leaves an inheritance to his children's, children".

So, this journal is dedicated to you!

I love you, yes even before you were ever born.

With love G'Ma Nikki

To my babies.....

Chris, Tay'vion, Tiarra, Torey and D2 y'all inspire me daily to PUSH beyond my limits and give me a reason to never settle for what this world will try to give.

BE DIFFERENT!

Love mama

To My Dearron......

Thank you for showing up and shaking up my life. Your unconditional love, support and encouragement is what I needed all along. I love you!

Your Wife

THE STORY OF YOUR LIFE WILL HAVE MANY CHAPTERS. DON'T GET STUCK IN THE ONE YOU'RE IN NOW.

God pick up the pieces.
Put me back together again.
You are my praise!

Jeremiah 17:14 MSG

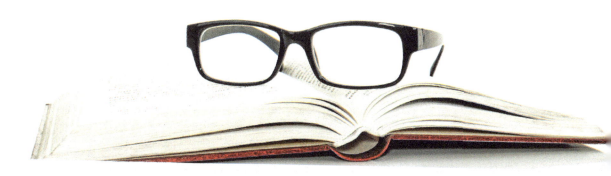

Let me take you back to a time, where I felt broken. Depending on when some people were introduced to me, it may appear that I woke up like this (in my Beyonce's voice) Nope! I had to work extremely hard to be the person I'm becoming now. My growth and joy began when I felt alone and fearful. I felt like I couldn't do life for many years. I worried about what others would say and I didn't want to let myself down as I tried to take on so may emotions. In 2012, when I lost my mom to Lung Cancer I was confused, hurt, annoyed and ALONE, in certain moments , so I thought. My heart was hardened, felt ripped out and completely out of order. There were days I wouldn't get up. I could hear someone talking to me, I would smile, yet not let a word make it beyond my ears. My kids would try to get me out of bed, my oldest even told me , "Ma, maybe you need a baby." lol. Ladies, I was broken to pieces. If you've ever lost a loved one then you know this feeling. However, as the years went by I got better, I began running towards God, in and out of church, therapy, going out, drinking you name it I was doing it.

My heart was searching for unconditional love while all along, Jesus was doing his big one behind the scenes and on the inside of me. I had no clue why I felt like breaking free at times would free ME.

Little did I know God was putting me back together again. Ladies, you can be both a work in progress and a masterpiece at the same time. READ THAT AGAIN!

Start healing, God is molding you into his perfect masterpiece. He sees your tears and as long as you have enough energy and courage to get up and take a step he will guide you into his arms.

Take 1 min and really get quiet, say OUT LOUD…

God, search my heart! Whatever just came to your mind first (Holy Ghost) is what he wants you to recognize.

God I feel

This is your chance to write your feelings down...

Write a letter to a loved one who is no longer with you physically (trust me it helps).

When we hide behind our smile, our children, our spouse, our jobs or even our past we delay the growth God has for us. Have you ever felt stuck or uncomfortable? If the answer is Yes, that's because we all have a purpose and God has downloaded fruits of his spirits into us. Galatians 5:22-23 Love, Joy , Peace, Patience, Kindness, Goodness, Faithfulness, Greatness and Self Control. So when we act outside of the spirit it feels uncomfortable. I've found that masking how you feel will hurt you more than help you. REMOVE your mask, because it's not meant to be worn everywhere! Especially when you're with the people God has placed in your life. Trust GOD! I myself had the hardest time with this one, if I felt my happy mask sliding I would quickly remove myself from you. Guess what ,it delayed my growth because Jesus sends us people to help uplift, encourage, deliver and bring us closer to him. How will anyone recognize you, if you have on a "mask". Be authentic and allow God to put your broken pieces back together!

Today I will be authentic with God

Staying stuck isn't an option this year, God is ready for you to live on purpose. He is looking for bold vessels.

What are you healing from?

How do you feel taking off your mask with God?

_____

_____

_____

_____

_____

I recognize my hurt and I give it all to you God promptly.

Here's some affirmations to say out loud daily: (add some personal ones)

I am Fearless
I am courageous
I am Bold
I am Strong
I am willing to grow
I am willing to learn
I am open to receive all that God has for me.
I am deserving
I will live with purpose and passion

Personal Affirmations:

Began seeking God first, everyone has a story or reason why they act or do the things that they do. It's up to you to recognize where you are broken, give it to God and allow him to start putting the pieces back together.

What part of my identity do I feel is broken?

Notes

Notes

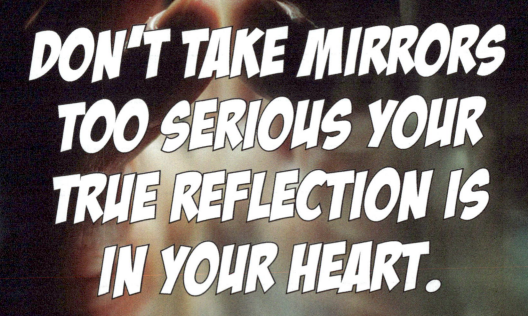

Search me, O God, and know my heart: Try me, and know my thoughts: And see if there be any wicked way in me, And lead me in the way everlasting.

Psalms 139:23-24 KJV

Ask yourself, WHO.AM .I? (pause) What do I like? What's my favorite color? What kind of car do I like? I know what you're thinking. Girl, what does this have to do with anything? I said the same thing when I was asked these exact questions years ago. I actually knew very quickly what I wanted or so I thought. LOL Let me explain, I'm a visual person so I knew I loved the color white. I knew that one day my closet will be filled with all white clothes. I knew what kind of house I wanted in full detail with the tall ceilings, my back wall would be windows, and a fireplace in my bedroom. You follow me. However, I was asked why? Why do you want those things, well well well, I didn't have a solid answer. I don't know, "it's cute", was my response. It was all surfaced. That's how most of us think, surfaced. We are geared to like most things that we see on social media or maybe what someone else have or wants. We even like things that are on someone else, never having a real reason for WHY. It's time to Dig a little deeper and to ask God to show you why! Why do I want or even like these "things" let me give you my personal example. My dream car was a G- Wagon and I wanted one so bad. When I did this exercise of my mind and heart, God revealed to me that it was to show off there was no real reason why I wanted that truck. There are other vehicles that I liked a lot more, but I wanted to flex it wasn't a dream car at all. Showing off and actually really liking a car are two different things. Flexing isn't pleasing to God nor is it aligned with the will he has set for you. Let's go deeper. Are you a person that gets frustrated when questioned ?Do you get mad, or maybe defensive if someone tries to have a deep conversation with you? Oh, here's a good one, do you avoid people all together? Ladies, being mean and isolating yourself will not get your point across because it is not God's will. There's always a deeper reason WHY you are acting out or shutting people out. Would you agree? God has created you for a purpose and once you realize what that purpose is you will begin making the necessary corrections. Always question YOURSELF (Flesh) Ask God to search your heart and remove anything that isn't of him.

Try to always adjust your thoughts and any of your ways that aren't aligned with your life!

How's my attitude normally?

_____

_____

_____

_____

_____

_____

What traits do I need to change?

_____

_____

_____

_____

_____

_____

How Do I view myself?

_____

_____

_____

_____

_____

_____

Remember to Ask God how he views you.
Isaiah 43:4

_____

_____

_____

_____

_____

_____

Trust me, it's not always easy knowing or should I say not knowing what you feel about yourself. We dress up, get our hair, nails ,brows done. I mean baby we will workout to death (I know I was there) Only to still see ourselves through the same eyes.

It's going to take HEART WORK!

Each morning for 3 days before the makeup , lashes and hair is applied. Take a look at your heart each day and ask God what should I give up today? Trust that he will guide you but actually do the work and go without "it."

Embrace YOU without anything extra.

Day 1. Today I will go without

_____

_____

_____

_____

_____

_____

Day 2. Today I will go without

Day 3. Today I will go without

True Story

I remember going to church and hearing "come as you are" I've always thought, they were talking about your attire or even if you have gone out the day before. Although those may be true as well, I truly believe God wants us to bring our HEART to him "AS IS" so that he can bring us to everlasting life.

What's on my heart

"_____

_____

_____

_____

_____

_____"

Notes

Notes

Notes

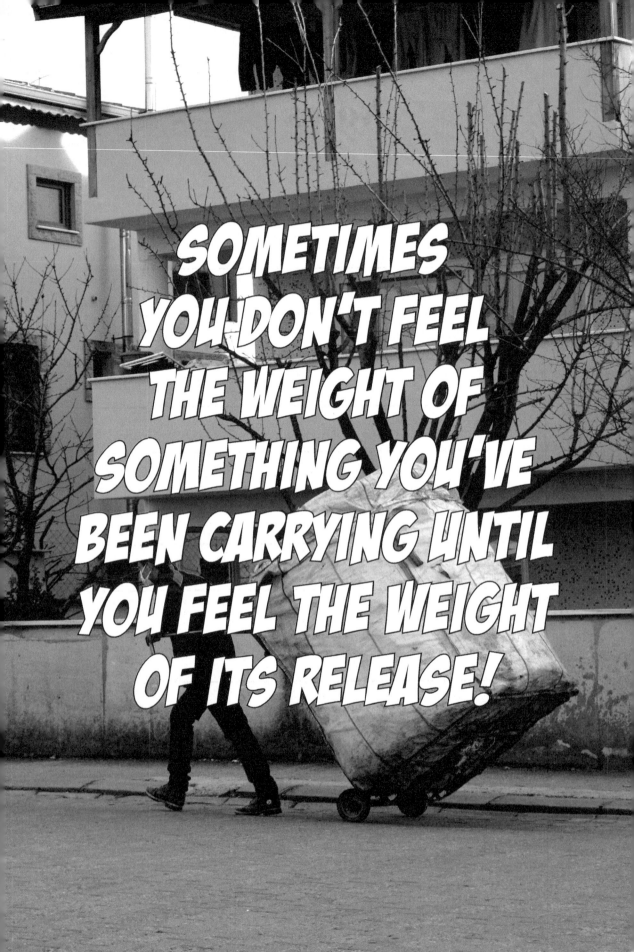

"Now I will take the load
from your shoulders;
I will free your hands from
their heavy tasks.

Psalms 81:6 NLT

What an honor it is to be labeled as the strong friend, daughter, mother , co worker etc. Ladies, we do a lot let me start off by saying be proud of yourself for all that you do for everyone else! We wear being strong as a badge of honor at times. Physically and mentally, we multitask like none other. Often we forget about ourselves! Why do you think we do this? Is it because we have seen our moms , grandmas and great aunts being forced to be strong and carry the weight of the family. What about the ladies who didn't have an example of strength but wanted to be independent . Either way let me tell you this. Give that weight to GOD. He wants us to cast all of our cares , worries and anxiety on him. He never created us to go through life ALONE or have to carry the weight of others. . Yes, sis you can put the weight of the family down , yup the kids and husbands , the divorce too, oh and don't forget the guilt.

Say this prayer:

Father God search my heart and remove from me any worry, doubt, or feelings of guilt. I give those things to you father God, the heaviness I have carried from childhood, a divorce, being a mom, even a friend, strengthen me in you oh God for it is too much for me to carry alone, So I give it all to you oh God. Amen

This small Prayer will hold a-lot of weight. So be sure to repeat it as often as needed.

What worries do you have? What am I anxious about? (List them)

Ask God to release you from the bondage of all those things. Ask him for help and allow you to be receptive to the help that he provides.

Do This:

Breathe in through your nose and out through your mouth (repeat as many times as needed)

Yup I know, the weight is lifted. Grab your spouse or son and have him do this with you. Men are not exempt, there's a lot they carry as well. Being the provider, protector and expected to show up in a certain way. My husband made me see things differently when it came to this. Maybe he will write a book for the fellas one day!

However, this allows you to feel the release of the weight being put down.

What's on my heart

"_____

_____

_____

_____"

Imagine yourself as THE BEST VERSION OF YOU and BECOME HER! How do you see yourself?

(place a picture of yourself below)

Notes

Notes

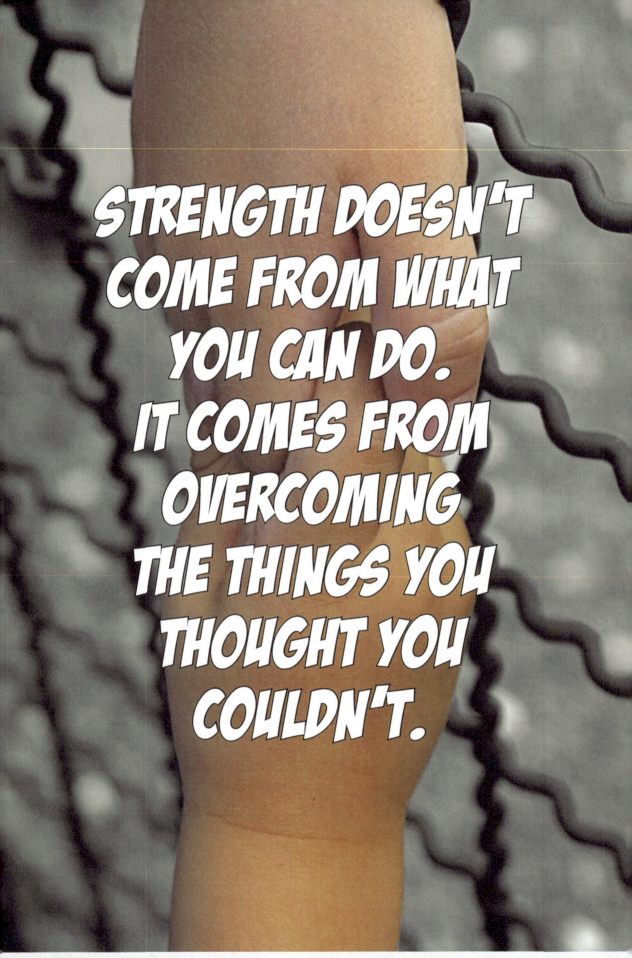

Come unto me, all ye that labour and are heavy laden, and I will give you rest.

Matthew 11:28 KJV

Where are my ladies that work out? Or want to workout? This one's for you! We all start out small maybe walking , jogging, then we graduate to lifting weights. Being able to do crazy exercises like holding a 40lb chain rope around your neck while balancing on a bosu ball doing squats will make you stronger. HA. Oh, wait that's just the day I felt extra strong. Let me paint this picture for you. I would wakeup at 3am pray and drive for about 30 min , meet my trainer, do all these extravagant workouts like the one I mentioned. Sessions were 1 hour , I would get pumped up just to drive home crying and feeling extremely weak, I did this for months ladies. My body was looking and feeling good, don't forget strong but my soul was weak. Can you relate? Being on a rollercoaster of emotions feeling strong and then a few minutes later feeling weak. My thoughts were all over the place. Ladies, my spirit couldn't lift a 5lbs dumbbell. I'm here to tell you, YOU NEED REST! Physical rest and spiritual strength is what's needed! You need to lift the BIBLE, get around ppl who lift your spirit. The exterior matters but your spirit will last far longer. You will have to figure out how to rest in a world that is so demanding of you. It's possible. Don't feel guilty for resting when needed. There will be meetings, deadlines, kids, husbands, and those so called girlfriends, demanding attention. I've found waking up before everyone helps to mentally prepare. your soul REST! Often trying to keep up with the times and escaping to the gym was my self care, but it did nothing to the problems. I found that what was needed was spirit care. Have you ever felt disconnected FROM the world the more you are IN the world? Well it's because your spirit is weak and empty, you can't pour from an empty cup. A daily recharge is necessary in order to get strong enough to face the highs and lows that comes with being human. Just like lifting weight you can't move on to the next weight size unless you put the other weight down and REST in between.

Physical and mental Rest equals Spiritual strength. Are you thinking, Nikki I have so much on my plate, how can I rest?

Guess what, even Jesus rested in order to be refueled to do BIG things in this world.

It's necessary Boo.

LOOK at your calendar when you add self care to it, don't go to the nail shop or hair appointment. Cancel everything and REST take your bible, or find a good book, listen to an inspirational podcast and grab this Years Journal. REST in the LORD because he has BIG PLANS for you. More than you could probably imagine. I'm here to tell you, you will need spiritual strength to complete any assignment he have in your life!

My REST DAY is scheduled for:

My favorite Bible verse is:

I'm grateful for:

_____

_____

_____

_____

_____

_____

What's on my heart

"_____

_____

_____

_____

_____"

Notes

_____

_____

_____

_____

_____

_____

_____

_____

_____

_____

_____

_____

Notes

NEVER LET YOUR FIRE GO OUT

Let your light so shine before men, that they may see your good works, and glorify your Father which is in heaven.

Matthew 5:16 KJV

It's really easy to take the backseat, turn your light off and forget who you are in certain situations. Especially in situations that you don't feel qualified to be in. Let me tell you, Don't you dare dim your light! I know that's easier said than done right? I've struggled with this one on and off my entire life. Public speaking, Whew chillleeeee, this one gets me every time. I've always been a person that loves to talk, make people laugh but when it comes to facing a huge crowd intimidation would set in. By now you can tell that I'm a person who knows the power of getting to the root of an issue. I honestly feel that's the only way to get rid of it. So, I went back to when I was a little girl, my mom would make my cousin and I read the King James Version of the Bible, if we argued or fought we knew what our punishment was , READ THE BIBLE! I used to feel like that was the Bible of all Bibles, because it was so hard for me to comprehend. I can still hear her at times "you can fight and argue but you can't read or pronounce that word"? Why did that stick with me for so long? I finally figured it out.

Because the enemy is a trickster. I was in elementary and middle school at the time of her saying this, surely it shouldn't be an issue in my adult life? Guess what? It was. I would shy away from reading out loud or speaking in crowds because I continued to hear those "hurtful" comments. The comments were never meant to be hurtful but my mom was very direct. Her point was meant for us to STOP fighting. However, that's how the enemy operates, he wants to kill, steal and destroy your mood, growth or anything. Any creativity, success and growth that may call for you to walk with a purpose he wants to take it away from you. What are you carrying from your past, that an elder has said that you are still holding on to today? Let It GO! God created us wonderful and in his image so why not allow your light to shine, for his glory! Negative thoughts will come to mind first, but those are just thoughts that didn't dawn on me until I was older. Telling myself girl, your mom making you read the Bible was not punishment but in fact getting you closer to God. Not knowing as of 2012 I would be facing the world without her. Ladies as long as you allow the enemy to distract you, he will. God is looking for bold vessels that will work through their insecurities and anytime he needs to appear through you for someone else. Think about it, why are you so nervous and afraid of certain things that elevate you? Like at church when they call you up for prayer no one goes really but we don't mind standing in a long club line. See! Mine was public speaking, yours might be meeting new people, writing your book, starting that business or leaving a toxic relationship. There's something holding you back from where God is calling you to go. That fire on the inside of you has to be ignited again. You will have to dash some gasoline on it. When I say dash gasoline I mean some motivation, inspiration and drive. Get close to God!

Surround yourself with people who pour into you. We all fall short and you will slip but when you do there has to be someone there to encourage you. Reminding you of what thus says the Lord. Keep that fire lit!

What are some hurtful words I was told about myself

"_____

_____

_____

                                                                    "
_____

How you see yourself is important.

What are some positive things I like about myself?

"
_____

_____

_____"

In order for you to ignite that fire, you must put out all low- self-esteem, insecurities, doubt, and trust issues with a bucket full of FAITH. It's going to require you to speak life over yourself.

Remember you are God's Girl the world is waiting for you , STAY LIT!

What's on my heart

"
_____

_____

_____

_____"

Notes

Notes

> More than anything you guard, protect your mind, for life flows from it.
>
> **Proverbs 4:23 CEB**

READ THE ENTIRE BOOK OF PROVERBS

You will find it to be the guide to life in all areas Faith, Finances, Relationship and most importantly Spiritually!

When you hear the word guard, what comes to mind? Protecting or covering comes to my mind. I visualize someone standing at a door (bouncer) with a blank stare watching out for who's coming in and out of a building with arms folded, someone stiff . If your visual is similar , you're right! Guard is to watch over or shield from danger or harm. So, there's no coincidence God instructs us to guard our minds. He wants us to keep certain things OUT so that we don't harm our hearts or minds. Stay with me, have you ever had a friend, family member or co- worker that may use profanity and when you are around you begin to use their language. YUP we all know someone, shoot we may be that person. How about a spouse you are around or best friend? Maybe even that co- worker that you talked with for 8 hrs you began to use the same words, slang or lingo as them. No worries, it's all normal. What goes in our minds, by sight or hearing, comes out. Good in, Good out , Bad in BAD OUT (think about it like that). It works the same way for faith and boldness about the word of God. When others begin to speak faith and do good deeds around you, watch how you pick up on that. Have you ever been in a drive through and someone says the car infant of you paid for your food? With no hesitation you probably said I'll pay for the car behind me. That's how it works, it's all returned 10 fold. Per God. My question is why don't we remember that even when we are around negativity. For example: If someone is using profanity or gossiping to you, I remember putting my two cents in on those conversations. No that's when we should remember to guard our mind so that our hearts are pure of any hurt, harm or disappointment. We should always be about business and remember what goes in, comes out. That goes for listening to music or watching certain TV shows that use language that are no longer serving on your new journey. I believe that God is just trying his best to protect us, would you agree?

What are some habits you want to break

Breaking habits will not be easy, as humans we are always ready to go back to our default or what's normal for us. Protecting your mind and heart will be a forced habit and require work. I've learned that you must be intentional and use the word of God as your shield. Put more good in although some things may be out of your control but that's when your disciplines will kick in.

I will replace all my old habits with

God is holding you accountable and he has given you the choice. You will have to be on watch for distractions and anything you listed will try its best to sneak past the guards. Remember to guard your mind at all costs especially if you want a fruitful life.

What's on my heart

Notes

Notes

NOTHING CHANGES IF NOTHING CHANGES

Do not conform to the pattern of this world, but be transformed by the renewing of your mind. Then you will be able to test and approve what God's will is- his good, pleasing and perfect will.

Romans 12:2NIV

Have you ever heard someone say, "that's just the way I am"? I used to believe that statement! Ha. I assumed changing my attitude or doing something out of my normal routine was a bad thing. Come close. it's NOT! Ladies, we're often attached to habits, people or our environment without even realizing there's other ways to do things. We're groomed a certain way at birth from the holiday traditions, foods we eat , down to the way that we parent, our career paths and even religion.

Have you ever noticed that those patterns are never an issue until you're exposed to something different? Think about it for a second, as we get older we experience life through own on lenses. As our perspectives begin to change, here we go questioning everything we've been accustomed to. What have you did differently than anyone ever exposed you to before? Sis, I stopped eating meat (I know wow) it started off as merely a challenge that turned into a lifestyle change. I loved it, I felt amazing and my health was great! However, the lip smacking at brunch, the girl stop playing at holiday functions almost made me forget why I even decided to do the 30 day challenge to begin with. My mom passed away from Lung Cancer, my grandma from Ovarian Cancer, two aunts have Breast Cancer y'all I wanted change!

I didn't go around making a public announcement but I told myself nothing will change, unless I change. I didn't want those generational illnesses to carry on to my kids. That's exactly what I thought to myself, girl give yourself and future generations a chance to see something different. Do you know that's how the enemy works when it comes to transforming and renewing your mind? He will cause you to only view negativity from the unknown and out of fear we stay the same for years. It is clearly written and "do not conform to the world." God has big things in store for us so we must shed away old ways and habits.

I only give one example here but the pressure to conform to worldly habits that may not be God's Law, is louder than ever these days. God sent Jesus as a sacrificial example of how we as people should act or respond to worldly experiences. Pay attention! Don't delay your transformation and the fear of not having a support system is okay, trust me although you may feel alone and like you're the only one in your circle changing, your appointed people are waiting on you. Change isn't always sudden; it will happen at different times for different people. Yes, it gets lonely walking the opposite way of the world, not going to parties, ordering water when you really want a cocktail. Okay okay that's just me LOL. Change starts as a thought or desire then action, a whole lot of faith and tons of Jesus. Have you thought about your purpose or asked God what must I change to fulfill my purpose? Remember, as you start to ask questions, he will start revealing to you in uncomfortable ways, pushing you to change. Embrace it!

Sit quiet for 5min.

What is my purpose?

What changes do I need to make to see a transformation?

BE OPEN and PIVIOT if needed. I won't lie it will be scary but so worth it.

I'm really good at

Father God I will not be conformed to this world if I have to stand alone I will do just that oh God. If I have to be the first to do it , I will be open to being THE BLUEPRINT, father God. When the world tells me to go left I will go right , right in your word oh God. I will consult with you before I make any decision, Father God . I trust you oh God although I don't like change but HERE WE GO!

What's on my heart

Notes

Notes

Notes

On the last and greatest day of the festival, Jesus stood and said in a loud voice,
"Let anyone who is thirsty come to me and drink. Whoever believes in me, as Scripture has said, rivers of living water will flow from within them."

John 7:37-39 NIV

I haven't always been a BIG believer. When I started to grow my faith, my belief level increased. Sis, It didn't happen all at once it was a slow process , or should I say it's an ongoing process from event to event. True story. I went back to work after being self-employed for about 3 years. I was told they would need me for 3 days ONLY! Well, well that 3 day need quickly transitioned to 6 months of employment.

If you've ever been an entrepreneur then you know I wasn't happy at all. I felt like I was going backwards, but I knew God had me there for a reason. I had no clue of what he was doing, I just felt it! I had to do some things I would have never agreed to like being a janitor. Girl sweep the floor , clean bathrooms, take orders that was just some of the things I did. However, I decided because God sent me I would serve until I was instructed otherwise.

Word of advice: your faith will grow outside of your comfort zone. You must believe that what Jesus told you will happen no matter how ugly the situation is.

This job increased my belief level more than any other time in my entire life... I worked many different roles there, so between there and personal training I was never STILL! Until I sat at the front desk, I was always made to think moving around was work. That was only half the truth. So, when this job required me to sit for periods of times, I would say, Nikki, you need to still be productive. One day, bored out of my mind, I decided to read a few pages of the book Crazy Faith by Micheal Todd. If you haven't read that book before go grab it or the audio. While reading "something" said to make that call. Well, let me take you back really quick. I have always wanted to personal train at a Women's facility or a homeless shelter. Everyone told me due to covid-19 no one will let me train at those facilities, so I never went forth with the idea. Until that day. Listen, has God ever given you instructions to do something that you desired but didn't do because of what someone said? I sure hope not. When God gives you a desire BELIEVE in it. I called 2 places both places said "yes, we've looked for someone to train our ladies and us too but haven't been successful." I was speechless!

God you mean to tell me all I had to do was call them? The Woman's Home emailed me the paperwork and guess what I did? You may be thinking I filled it out and emailed it right back. Nope, I was so in Aww of what God did...it took me 3 months or more to fill the paperwork out. LOL y'all If God tells you to do something he's waiting on you to do it. He will prepare everything for you to walk in it. Believe, but you must take action in what God tells you. Fast forward I met some amazing ladies at that facility. I was able to help them with using some of these same concepts and tools that God used to help guide me through dark times. I still keep in contact with some of them as well. That event happened and guess what it did , it strengthened my belief. It was right there in scripture this entire time. I have many more stories where God showed up just by me accepting a job doing things I had never imagined.

I would joke with the ladies that the building was covered by the blood of Jesus, seriously when you're ready Jesus appears. I would have never experienced the spirit in that way or delayed my time to meet those ladies if I had not taken action. Experiences, Belief, Faith, Action all goes hand in hand. Faith is to believe what you cannot see. Do you have Faith in that.

I'm believing God for (Crazy Faith)

_____

_____

_____

_____

_____

_____

Journaling is a way to bring your desires to life.

God has instructed me to:

_____

_____

_____

_____

_____

_____

I dare you to PIVOT. Do something you have never done before.

Accept a job while you still have your business.

Call that place that you are scared to hear no from.

Call that friend that you lost touch with.

Change careers.

Start a business. Leave that house.

MOVE.

Believe and watch God increase your belief level and grow your faith.

What's on my heart

"_____

_____

_____

_____

_____

_____"

Notes

Notes

Notes

Make no mistake, God is not mocked. A person will harvest what they plant. Those who plant only for their own benefit will harvest devastation from their selfishness, but those who plant for the benefit of the Spirit will harvest eternal life from the Spirit.

Galatians 6:7-8 CEB

Ladies, have you ever thought to yourself, I'm going to be rich one day? As a kid I bet many of us had those same thoughts. The vision of having a big house, fancy cars, our own version of what we thought success looked like. As we get older that version of our life, the tangible things we once desired may not come to mind as much. They do still show up for me, I'm reminded whenever I participate in any vision board party. Lol have you ever associated being blessed or what blessings should look like with "things." ? I know I have, I would look at someone's "things" and even my own and feel like, oh God you are really blessing us. Oh boy was I wrong. There I was thinking surfaced again. We're taught to work a good job to make a lot of money so we're able to buy those nice things, right? Until you have those "things" but often feeling unsatisfied. It's just never enough. Sis, one day the Holy Spirit said , "Nikki what are you investing to really get anything in return? And I'm not talking about money or objects. made me constantly think, NO INVESTMENT NO RETURN.

That stuck with me so I began to change my mindset. The big picture, what is it that you really want Nikki? So, I will ask you What is is that you really want? Nope it cant be money or anything money can buy. Hmmmm it may take a minute. Take your time! I realized that the best investment would be in myself and my family. Rather it was my time, my money, reading books , eating healthier , working out or even finding self development events to attend, I knew I had to invest more in myself. I expected more SPIRITUALLY. Sis, whatever area you want to see a return in you must invest in it, that became a way of life for me.

I will invest in

----

to see a return in

God is waiting to see how you will invest your love, joy and faith.

Do not think you can cheat God he knows if we're really investing. He's not going to give us more than we put in, he's not going to allow us to be blessed with bad intention.

These investments are being deposited into heaven keep making those positive INVESTMENTS!

What's on my heart

"_____

_____

_____

_____

_____

_____"

Notes

Notes

Notes

YOUR STORY IS CHANGING

Forget the former things; do not dwell on the past. See, I am doing a new thing! Now it springs up; do you not perceive it? I am making a way in the wilderness and streams in the wasteland.

Isaiah 43:18-19 NIV

Change. It's something we've all said that we wanted at some point in our lives but were rarely ever 100% ready to do what it took to see a real change. Have you ever asked God for something that requires you to make some changes? Then you took your time changing and blamed the delay on God, like you were waiting on him? LOL think about it. I've been guilty of asking Jesus for certain things as well knowing if he gave them to me right away I wouldn't know what to do with them. Elevation and most things we ask God to do for us WILL require CHANGE. So, prepare now! I've found out that God wants us to bring praise to his name more than anything else, the way we act or heart posture we make are for God's glory. Let me share with you my perspective regarding change. An invisible box will be placed around your life that is stopping you when you are not obedient to change. Limitations. What limitations have you placed on your life? Sis, my invisible box was "Justfitnikki". trust me, it can be removed and adjusted at any time, that's the cool part. You hold the tool box to make the necessary changes! But newsflash YOU will have to make the necessary changes. For me, I wasn't even aware that I was creating borders, you probably won't either, that's why I'm sharing this with you, in hopes that you avoid or remove sooner. Unlike me I was allowing my life to be centered around working out due to the success and the praise others would give me. I assumed God told me to be a personal trainer all because of a name I was given and my ability to easily help others see results in that area. However, it stopped me from learning or doing anything beyond health and wellness. One day I heard very clear instructions to change my name. I was so shocked when I heard that voice in my head. Listen, when I read that Jesus called his disciples by name in Luke 6;12-16 was all the confirmation needed.

God chose his disciples, Simon he called Peter; Andrew he called James and the list goes on. Now it was my turn , Justfitnikki he called LaTosha, someone who didn't just personal train but was open to other opportunities that allowed her to do God's will as he saw fit. Making changes will demand a shift in all areas or a delay. It's our choice! Grab the hammer like I had to do and when I say hammer I mean my Instagram name, and remove it. Listen, God may have you change something so simple as your hair, your job or your furniture , for me it was my social name, whatever it looks like REMOVE IT. Those simple changes cause limitations. You will never grow like the shark in a fishbowl.(look up that story) You will have to break free and make space for God to work in your life. ARE YOU READY FOR CHANGE? WILL YOU BE OBEDIENT? Here's your chance. You don't have to make a public announcement, just like weight loss, It will take some time: 4 weeks you will notice wow i'm changing. 8 weeks people who are close to you began to notice a change and 12 weeks the world sees but most importantly God sees the day by day changes that you decided to take.

Keep making changes because NOTHING CHANGE IF CHANGES!

What have you built a wall/limitations around in your life:

_____

_____

_____

_____

How do you plan on removing the limits:

How do you feel about embracing change:

Forget the past but never forget those lessons or experiences you've learned along the way. You have permission to change and not be held hostage.

What's on your heart

"_____

_____

_____

_____

_____

                                    "
_____

Take a deep breath, this journal was written with your growth in mind. If you have ever felt stuck, lost , hurt after experiencing a loss, lonely or discouraged this will serve you as a guide to let go, you are not alone. Helping you really release those emotions one day at a time.

These real life situations, advice, quotes and scriptures that I share have helped me and others navigate back to God. You will have to learn to lean on him, not friends or family. It will be tough at first. However, as God allows you to release trauma that you battle as you journal, he will restore comfort, peace and joy. Get ready and EXPECT to attract new opportunities, love , community and power.

Be encouraged Boo.

Love ya!

Remember when life is pressuring you, think about your future and PRESS FORWARD!

Here's a few quotes that have helped me that I've picked up along the way.

Sis, remember you are braver than you believe.

Your emotions affect your energy, energy affect your productivity.

Live in the now!

Always remember God has created you for a purpose and reason.

YOUR LIFE MATTERS!

Notes

Notes

Notes

Notes

Notes

Notes

Notes

Notes

Notes

Notes

Notes

Notes

Notes

Notes

Notes

Notes

Notes

Notes

Notes

Notes

Notes

Notes

Made in the USA
Columbia, SC
08 February 2025